CONTENTS

Some materials you will need

Pieces of felt

Pieces of Binca canvas

Small amount of check gingham (5 squares=3cm approx.)

A tapestry needle

A crewel embroidery needle

Coloured embroidery wool

Soft embroidery cotton

Coton à broder

A thimble (this should fit your middle finger)

A few pins

Cotton for tacking

A pair of scissors (small ones for cutting off thread etc.)
You will need your Mother's bigger scissors for cutting out material. Do ask before you take them.

Paper for making patterns (clean greaseproof paper will do)

Ruler

Tape measure

Buttons

Bodkin (to thread elastic)

Kapok

A chalk pencil (the dressmaking kind)

A little Copydex

Sewing

by NOREEN DAVIS

with illustrations by
ERIC WINTER

Ladybird Books Ltd Loughborough

Introduction

There are many kinds of needlework and much of it is done solely for pleasure. You will enjoy learning how to sew, and making the things in this book.

Before you begin, look at the list of the things you will need at the front of this book. Collect them together and keep them in a small cardboard box.

A thimble may be hard to get used to, but it does protect the middle finger which pushes the needle through the material. Before you buy one, try it on to make sure it fits.

Use scissors carefully. At first it would be wise to ask your mother to help you when cutting out material. When she sees how sensible you are, she will allow you to cut out on your own. Always cut out on a clean, uncluttered surface.

Pins, needles and scissors should always be put away as soon as possible after use.

You will be more pleased with the result if you have kept your needlework clean and tidy. Always work with clean hands. If they are not clean – wash them!

0 7214 0326 3

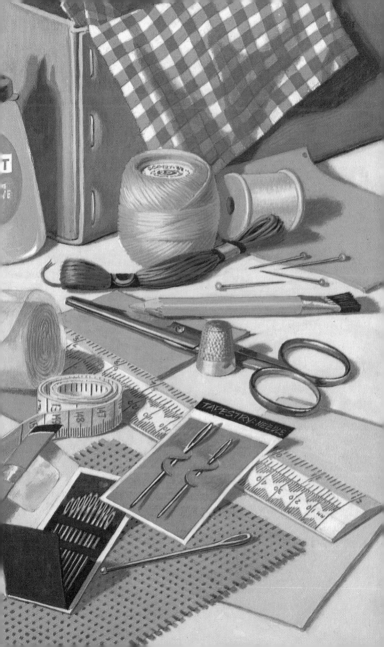

Making a table mat

To make this mat you will need:

A small piece of Binca canvas

Some coloured embroidery wool

A tapestry needle

The mat in the picture opposite is very simple to make.

Thread your needle and push it in one hole of the canvas and out of the next.

It is a good idea to begin with a straight line. Make a pattern with lines, using coloured embroidery wool. Trim all the long ends of the wool level with the canvas.

Maybe you would like to make more of these mats, trying various patterns, before you make other things.

Fastening on and off

When sewing, it is important to make both ends of your thread secure so that it will not come undone.

Fastening on and off should be done firmly and neatly. On Binca canvas you fasten on by putting the needle *between* two layers of threads *at the back* of the material. Make two stitches, one over the other. If you have done this correctly, these stitches will not show on the front of the material. Now push your needle through to the front, ready to begin sewing.

When you have finished your pattern or used up your thread, fasten off in the same way by pushing your needle through to the back and again making two small stitches between the threads as shown opposite (top). Trim off the ends of the thread.

Cross stitch

Cross stitch is quite easy if worked on Binca canvas or check material, as squares are already there for you to follow. The lower picture opposite shows how this stitch is made on check gingham. When making cross stitch on Binca canvas, as shown in the upper picture, a cross is made in alternate squares, and the resulting pattern is the same on both sides of the canvas.

Use a piece of Binca canvas and make a mat with a cross stitch pattern. Do not forget to fasten on and off.

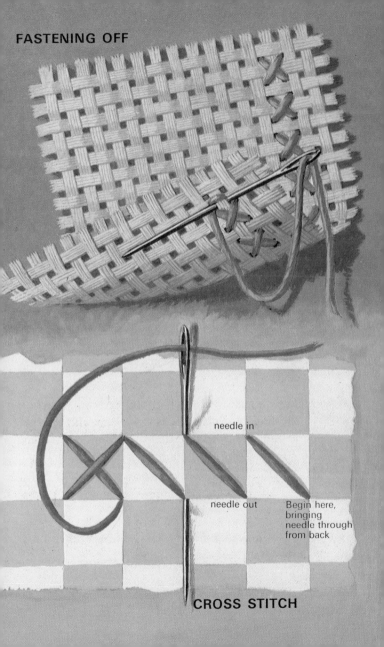

FASTENING OFF

needle in

needle out

Begin here, bringing needle through from back

CROSS STITCH

Practice with patterns

On the opposite page are some patterns which can be made on small pieces of Binca canvas or check gingham.

Try these patterns first on Binca canvas.

Nos. 1 and 2: Put your needle in one hole and out of the next in a straight line. Two rows will make a pattern.

Nos. 3 and 4: Each consists of two straight rows of stitches (as in No. 1) with part of the cross stitch in between.

No. 5: Two straight rows of stitches have cross stitches in between.

No. 6: This pattern is formed by two separate rows of stitches. Do the top row first, with the same stitch as in the centre of No. 3, then do the lower row with the same stitch as that in the centre of No. 4.

No. 7: This is made with two straight rows of stitches, the ends of each stitch being joined with another colour. You will find that there is more than one way of doing this joining.

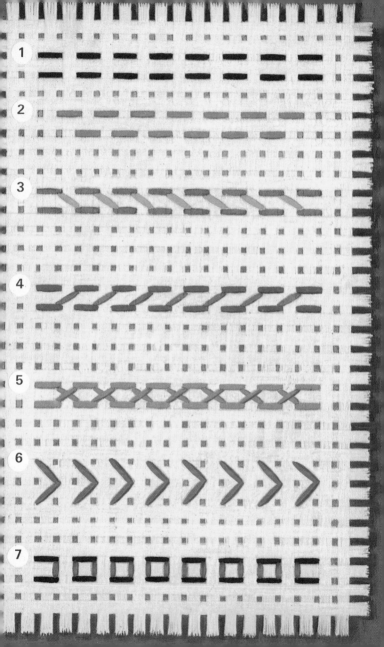

Making another table mat

You will need:

A piece of Binca canvas

Some embroidery wool or Anchor soft embroidery cotton

A tapestry needle

As these mats have no hems, it is best to leave a margin about the width of that shown in the picture.

Fasten on and off at the back of your work.

Work a border all round. Make this a simple one otherwise you might have difficulty in matching the corners. For this reason the rest of the pattern should be in straight rows. Use your colours carefully, trying one colour against the other before you begin.

You could make a mat to put under a vase of flowers or a small ornament.

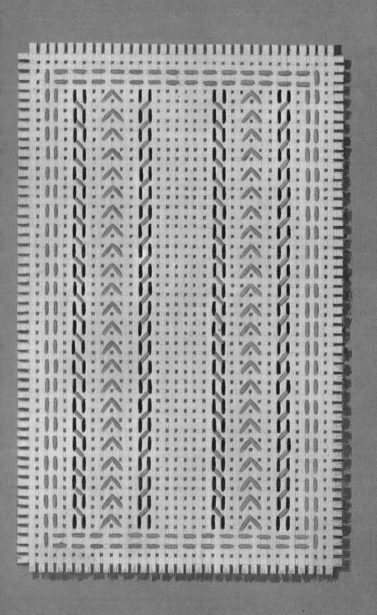

Various stitches

Running Stitch. This is the easiest stitch to make, and is the one shown on previous pages. All stitches should be even and equal in length.

Whipped Running Stitch. Begin with a line of running stitch using coton à broder on a piece of felt. Using another colour, pass the needle under each stitch from the top but not through the material. Do not pull the thread too tight.

Threaded Running Stitch. Begin with a line of running stitch using coton à broder on a piece of felt. Next pass the needle, threaded with another colour, down and under one stitch, then up and under the next. Do not go through the material, nor pull the thread too tight.

Oversewing. This stitch can be used to fasten one piece of material to another or to secure tapes. The stitches should be small, evenly spaced and close together. Do not pull the cotton too tight, and be sure to keep the two edges of the material level. Practise with two pieces of thin felt and coton à broder.

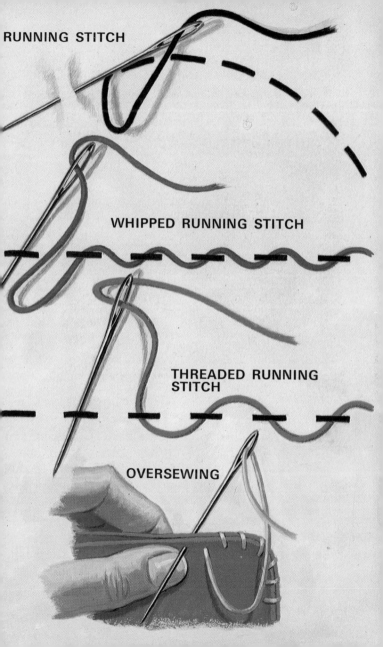

RUNNING STITCH

WHIPPED RUNNING STITCH

THREADED RUNNING STITCH

OVERSEWING

Making a pincushion

For this you will need:

Two 3″ (8cm) squares of felt

Another tiny strip of felt for the loop

Coton à broder

A needle

The pieces of felt can be the same colour, but felt of different colours can be used.

Draw a circle in the centre of one of the squares of felt, using a chalk pencil. This can be brushed off later. A tin lid about $2\frac{1}{2}$″ (6cm) across can be used as a guide.

Begin by sewing round the circle using running stitch. Do not pull this tight. Always fasten on and off. The running stitch can be 'whipped' using a different colour. Round off each corner of the felt squares by drawing partly round a coin or counter and then cutting along the line.

Pin the two pieces of felt together, putting the loop between and in one corner of the felt. Then tack the two pieces together. Oversew the two pieces together taking care to sew into each piece of felt. A few extra stitches will be needed to hold the loop firm. Leave 2″ (5cm) open on the last side.

Use kapok, or clean nylon stockings which have been cut up, to fill the pincushion until it is neatly rounded. Then oversew the gap.

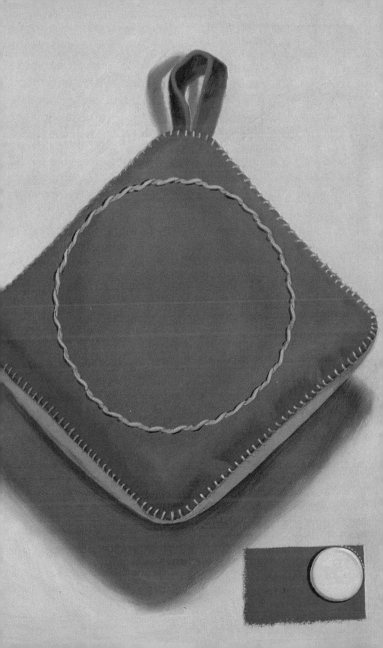

Sewing on a button

It is important to know how to sew on a button properly. First you must check that it is in the correct position and that you are sewing it onto a double thickness of material. If you use cotton it must be doubled. Button thread can be used singly.

Fasten on at the back of the material. Pass the needle through from the back of the material and through one of the holes of the button. Place a large pin over the front of the button and sew over this as shown opposite. When you have sewn it enough, remove the pin, pass the needle through a hole to the back of the button and then bind the thread several times round and round the 'stalk' of thread between the button and the material. Then take the thread through to the back of the material and fasten off.

Patterns can be made on a piece of thick material by stitching on buttons of different shapes and sizes. Ask your mother if you may have the buttons from clothes which are worn out. It is a good idea to make a collection of buttons.

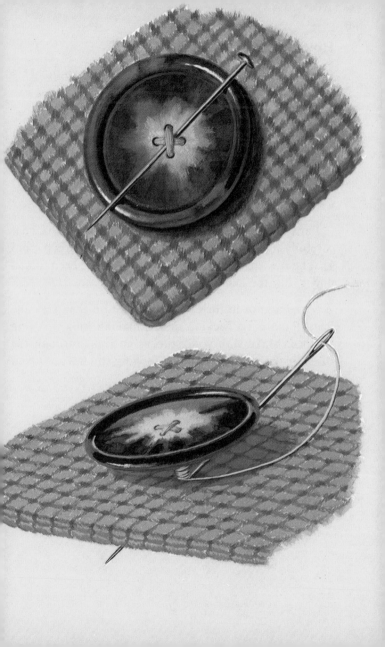

How to turn a hem

Make a cardboard guide like the one opposite. This helps to make sure the hem is level.

Draw a pencil line across the guide; this should be the depth of the first turning down of the raw edge and will help you to turn it down evenly. To do this, put the guide on the material, turning the material over it until the raw edge meets the line. Press along the folded edge with your thumb and first finger.

Turn down again, measuring the depth of the hem carefully against the cut edge of the guide (see Picture 1). The raw edge of the fabric will now have been folded under. Pin the hem down (Picture 2).

Make a knot in the end of your cotton then tack the hem (Picture 3). Tacking means making long, running stitches. Make sure your stitches go right through the three thicknesses of material. Tacking stitches are taken out when the sewing is completed.

Make sure the guide and hem are level

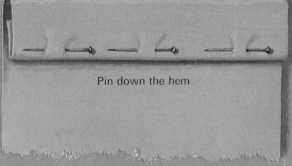

Pin down the hem

2

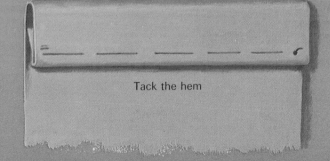

Tack the hem

3

Making a gingham mat or tray cloth

You will need:

A square of check gingham

Some tacking cotton

A few pins

A needle

Coton à broder

Each edge of the mat must have a hem if it is to wash and wear well. Carefully measure and turn down each side to make a hem. The hem must be turned down onto the side of the material which will face uppermost. Then pin and tack each hem.

Make a pattern along the edge of each hem, using running stitch or cross stitch. This will hold the hem down. Make sure you complete each side before you remove any tacking stitches.

Oversew each corner.

Use the squares as a guide to put a cross stitch pattern in the centre.

Making a jewellery pack

For this you will need:

Two circles of felt $2\frac{1}{2}''$–$3''$ (7cm–8cm) across the widest part

Two small leaf shapes cut from green felt

A bead

Coton à broder

This little pocket makes a very special small gift. Your mother, an aunty, grandmother or friends would be pleased to receive one. It can hold a brooch, ear rings, a small bottle of perfume, a lipstick or a tape measure and thimble. It could be used as a present for daddy with cuff-links, a tie clip or a map measure tucked inside.

Place the two small felt leaves on one circle of felt and sew down the two wider ends only. Sew a bead into the centre of the leaves.

Tack the two circles of felt together. Oversew the two sides together leaving about $2''$ (5cm) open.

Be sure to fasten on and fasten off securely.

A dressing-table set

You will need:

A piece of Binca canvas about 18″ x 12″ (45cm x 30cm)

Embroidery silk or cotton

Anchor soft embroidery or something similar

A tapestry needle

Cut one large mat 12″ x 12″ (30cm x 30cm). Then cut the remaining canvas into two equal pieces 6″ x 6″ (15cm x 15cm). These suggested sizes are a guide only. Any odd pieces of Binca canvas could be used.

Use any of the stitch patterns suggested earlier for Binca embroidery. Sew the large mat first. Stitch a pattern along one edge and match it on the opposite side. This is easier than trying to work right round the mat.

If you work in complete rounds, choose a simple pattern to begin with, then you will see whether your corners will match.

When the large mat is completed, the same pattern or part of the pattern, can be put onto each of the small mats.

Making a felt fish

You will need:

Two pieces of felt – different colours will do

A small strip of felt for the gusset if used

A needle   Coton à broder

Fold a piece of tracing paper. Lay the folded edge along the straight edge of Figure 1 and trace the shape. With the paper still folded, cut out the shape and then open it up. You will have a complete fish shape. Cut out two pieces of felt to the shape of the fish.

Sew a few stitches for an eye on each piece of felt. Another way of making an eye is to stitch on a small circle of felt. The decoration opposite can then be copied, or you can invent your own.

Place the two pieces of felt together with the eyes on the outside. Tack the pieces together and oversew, leaving a gap of 2″ (5cm). Using kapok, cotton wool, or clean nylon stockings (which have been cut up into small pieces) fill the fish until it is neatly rounded. Oversew the gap.

Your fish will be even more realistic if you use a gusset. To do this, fold a piece of tracing paper and lay the folded edge along Figure 2. Trace the shape and cut it out with the paper still folded. Open it up. Cut one piece of felt to the shape of the gusset.

Embroider your design on the two outsides of the fish. Take one half of the fish and lay point A of the gusset on point A of the inside of the fish and point B of the gusset on point B of the fish. Tack and oversew one edge of the gusset to one edge of the fish. In the same way, tack and oversew one edge of the other half of the fish to the other edge of the gusset.

Tack and oversew from point B round the tail and along the side of the fish, leaving a 2″ (5cm) gap. Stuff the fish through the gap and then close it by oversewing.

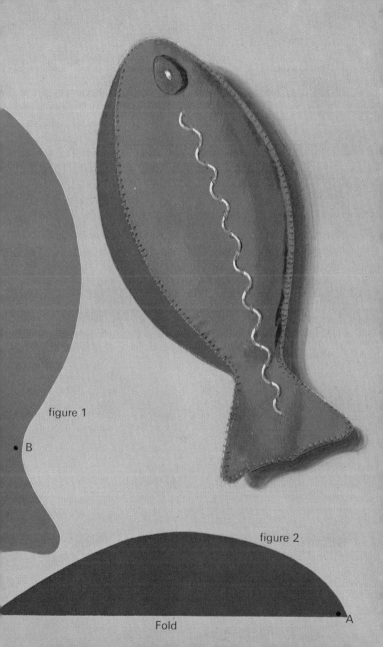

figure 1

• B

figure 2

• A

Fold

Two new stitches to learn

Chain stitch

The illustration opposite shows how this useful embroidery stitch can be done. Be careful not to pull the thread too tight. Practise with a piece of felt and coton à broder.

Blanket stitch

This stitch is often used to neaten a single edge or join two edges. The illustration shows how it is done. Stitch with edge towards you and work from left to right.

A chalk line, parallel to the edge of the material, will help you to keep your stitches even in length. To start, fasten on at the back of the material as near to the edge as possible, then put the needle in on the chalk line at the front.

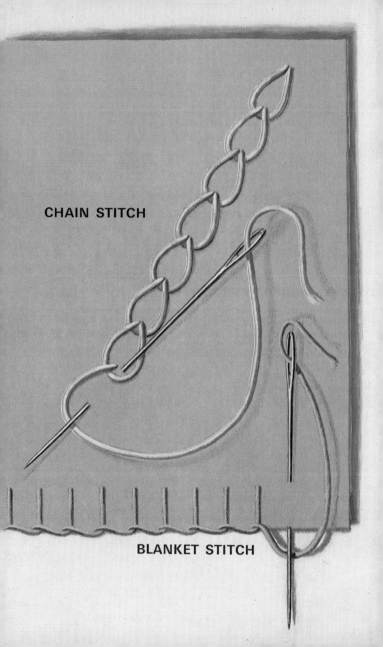

CHAIN STITCH

BLANKET STITCH

Making a comb case

Materials needed:

A strip of felt twice the length of the comb and a little wider

Embroidery thread

A needle

Stitch a design the whole length of the felt. To copy the design opposite, draw the straight lines with a ruler and a chalk pencil. Use a coin to help draw the semi-circles.

When you have stitched the design, fold the felt in half and round off the corners.

Pin the sides together and tack. Blanket stitch both long sides. Keep the top open, of course. The top edges can be blanket stitched separately to match the rest.

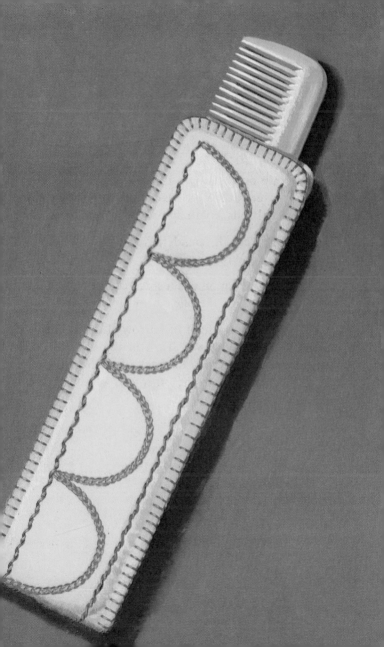

Making a hairband

You will need:

A piece of felt about 12″ (30cm) long and 2″ (5cm) wide

Some embroidery silk

A length of narrow elastic

To decide on the length of the hairband, ask some-one to measure over your head from ear to ear. Cut out a piece of felt this length and round off each corner.

Blanket stitch all round the edge of the hairband, fastening on and off neatly.

The centre design in chain stitch can be copied if you wish, or you can make one of your own choice.

To finish, cut a length of narrow elastic to hold the hairband neatly in place. Turn in the cut end of the elastic and oversew it to the back of the felt at one end of the hairband. Sew the other end of the elastic to match.

A round pincushion

You will need:

Two circles of felt

A small piece of felt or cord for a loop

Embroidery silk

A needle

Kapok

Cut out two circles of felt. You could draw round a cup, plastic beaker or a small tin lid to get a circle.

The design is worked first on one piece of felt. The design you choose could include several different stitches. The one opposite uses:

>Chain stitch
>
>Whipped running stitch
>
>Threaded running stitch
>
>Blanket stitch

When the design is finished, pin and tack the two circles of felt together. Put the loop into place with a few careful stitches and blanket stitch round the edge of the pincushion, leaving a space for the filling.

Fill the pincushion with kapok, cotton wool, or clean nylon stockings which have been cut into small pieces. Blanket stitch the remaining gap.

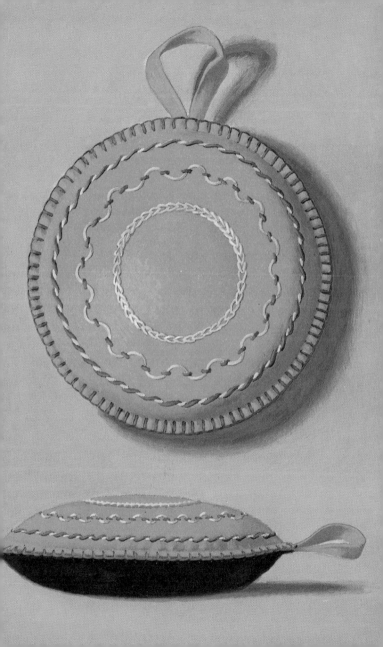

Making a needle case

You will need:

A piece of felt 7″ x 5″ (18cm x 12cm)

Some coton à broder or other embroidery silk

A piece of flannel or another piece of felt a little smaller than 7″ x 5″ (18cm x 12cm)

If you can borrow a pair of pinking shears from your mother, use these to cut out both the felt and the flannel. They make attractive edges like those in the picture.

If you are using two pieces of felt and ordinary scissors, cut out the felt and round each corner with the help of a coin. Copy the chain stitch design onto the felt, and use embroidery silk of different colours.

To make up:

Place the two pieces of felt, or the felt and flannel, together, one exactly on top of the other. Pin them together and sew down the centre in a straight line using small running stitches or back stitches. Make sure you stitch right through both thicknesses. Fasten off firmly.

Fold in half and the needle case now looks like a book.

Making a felt toy

For this you will need:

A picture

Two large pieces of felt

Small pieces of felt to decorate

Embroidery thread

A needle

A toy can easily be made using a picture traced from a birthday card or an outline from a painting book. Only the outline and the simplest details are needed.

You will find that a large, bold picture will be easier to work on than a tiny one.

Trace the picture onto a sheet of paper. Cut this out to make a paper pattern. Pin the pattern to the two pieces of felt and cut out carefully. Instead of pinning on the pattern you could draw round it if it is firm enough, and cut out the outline.

Mark the eyes, nose, etc., onto one piece of felt. Sew round these in running stitch, or make eyes and nose from scraps and sew these on.

Pin the two shapes of felt together, tack and then oversew. Leave 2″ (5cm) open on the side of the body.

Use kapok, cotton wool, or clean nylon stockings which have been cut up into very small pieces, to fill the shape till neatly rounded. Push the stuffing into the corners of the toy with a pencil. Oversew the remaining gap.

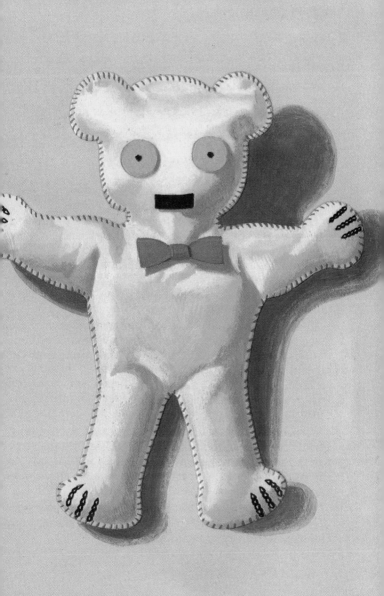

A felt purse

You will need:

A small piece of felt 5″ x 8″ (12cm x 20cm)

Some small pieces of felt to decorate

A few beads (these can be from a broken necklace)

Paper for patterns (greaseproof paper will do)

Coton à broder

Cut out the main piece of felt and round off both corners on one of the short sides. Fold in half the paper being used for a pattern. Open out again and place the fold line on the edge AB of the pattern opposite (Figure 1). Trace the outline of the pattern. Fold the paper again, and pin or glue together the corners of the two halves at the points marked in the diagram opposite. Cut around the outlines. You will now have four diamond shapes.

Place the diamond shapes in position on your main piece of felt and decide which colour felt to use for your design. Pin the paper shapes to the felt pieces and cut around them. Pin and tack them, or use a little adhesive to hold them in place. Using small stitches, catch the felt pieces to the purse. Make design (Figure 2) for purse flap in the same manner.

A bead can be sewn to the centre of each shape. Fasten on, sew on the bead, fasten off, then do the same for the next bead. This avoids having long threads on the back of the work. Tiny felt shapes in other colours can be used instead of beads.

Fold the purse into three. Pin and tack each side. Remove the pins. Blanket stitch each side and around the flap. Remove the tacking stitches.

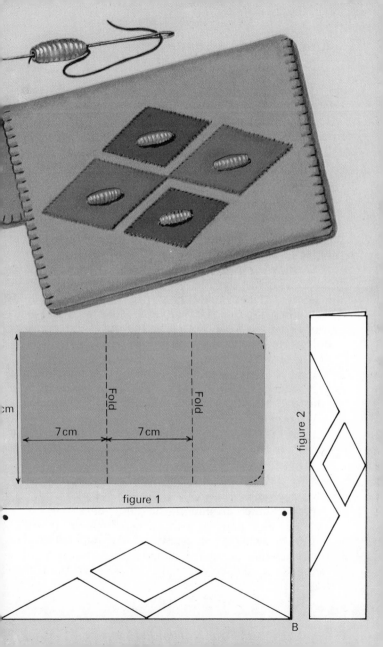

cm

7 cm | 7 cm

Fold | Fold

figure 1

figure 2

B

Making a doll's bonnet

You will need:

A piece of felt

Two long narrow strips of felt or
two pieces of narrow ribbon

Some embroidery silk

A needle

Paper for pattern

Make a paper pattern similar to the one opposite but
made to fit your doll.

To do this, measure round the doll's face to obtain
the measurement of the front edge of the bonnet. Draw
a line that length on some paper. Make a mark half-
way along the line. Draw another line from this half-
way mark the same length as the distance from your
doll's forehead to the back of her neck. The plan opposite shows you how.

Find the middle and then put (X) on this line and
draw the line A B X C D. Now draw the outline of
your pattern, the distances AB, BC and CD are equal.

When you have cut out your pattern, pin it onto the
felt and cut round the pattern. Round off the two front
corners of the felt and trim a little piece off each corner
at E and F as shown in the diagram.

Embroider a design similar to the one in the picture.

Oversew side AB to BE and side FC to CD.

Blanket stitch around all the outer edges.

Attach two long, narrow strips of felt or ribbon as
ties, oversewing these neatly to the under-side. The
ribbon should be folded under and oversewn and the
free ends should be cut diagonally to stop the ribbon
fraying.

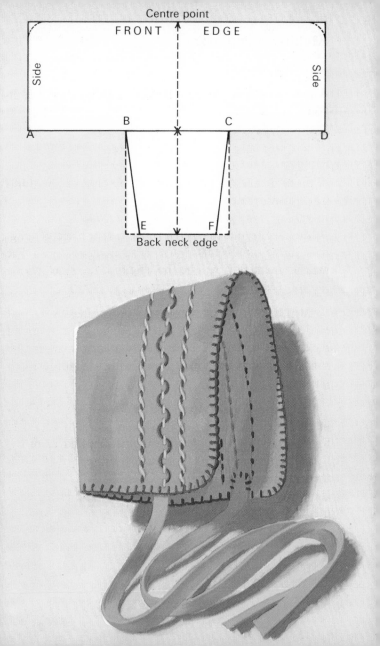

Centre point

FRONT   EDGE

Side

B   C

A   D

E   F

Back neck edge

Making a doll's skirt

Materials needed:

A piece of check gingham (the size can be altered to fit your own doll)

Some cotton, a few pins, a needle, a bodkin

Coton à broder

A piece of narrow elastic almost as long as the doll's waist measurement

Measure round the doll's waist. Cut a piece of gingham three times this waist measurement A–B. The measurement B–C will be the length of the skirt, allowing for a hem.

Turn down hems on the two short sides A–D and B–C. Do this on the right side of the gingham. Pin and tack. Turn down hems on the two long sides in the same way. Sew each hem down with a running stitch pattern.

Embroider a pattern on the one long side (D–C) as in the picture. Bring the two short sides of the skirt together and oversew, leaving the two end edges of the waist hem open. The elastic can be threaded through the waist hem with a bodkin. Oversew the two edges of the elastic and finish by oversewing the gap in the ends of the hem.

This length to be 3 times the doll's waist measurement.

B

C

A collage – an unusual kind of picture

Collect scraps of material of all kinds and shapes and sizes. They can be rough or smooth, plain or patterned. Your mother may have some which she can spare. Some shops make dress alterations and will let you have a bag of 'bits'. If you know a dressmaker she may give you some 'pieces'. These are ideal as they are new and often quite large.

It is useful to collect bits of braid, ribbon, binding, tape and pretty coloured string. Beads from broken necklaces, sequins and other decorations from old dresses can be useful. Collect buttons of all different shapes and sizes.

Decide which pieces of material you are going to use and ask your mother to press them to remove any creases. Cut them into interesting shapes of suitable sizes.

When you have enough, put a few of your pieces of material together on a piece of paper. Arrange them until you like the design you see. Then choose a piece of material for a background. Embroidery linen is ideal but can be expensive. For the background of the design shown opposite, coloured felt was used.

A collage – *continued*

Any material which frays will need to have a small amount turned under before it is stitched down. Some materials such as felt do not fray and do not need turning down.

Sew the pieces of material to the background. If you wish, you can embroider them first. Find pieces of ribbon or braid to sew over any rough edges. Sew on sequins or beads. When the picture is finished, mount on card (or use plastic strips for hanging posters). If you cannot get sequins or beads, look around for something else. Maybe your father can find you some tiny nuts or washers from his tool box. There is no limit to the things you can find to put in your picture.

If you find a lot, do not use them all at once. Make another picture. Pages 49 and 51 show the sort of 'collages' you can make.

Allow a wide margin on the outside of your picture if you wish to mount it on some card. The edges can be turned over the card and glued on the back, or stitched across from side to side with the corner folds stitched together.

Coloured hessian was used for the background of the picture opposite.

Making a sewing card

Sewing cards make good presents for younger children. You can make them quite easily. They can also be used for transferring patterns onto material for embroidery.

First look for a suitable picture to draw around. You need only an outline and the simplest details as in the picture opposite. Birthday cards, paintbook and magazine pictures can be used. Make sure the picture is bold enough to sew around.

Look for a piece of thin card or stiff paper. The plain side of food packets, post cards or the white card which comes in packets of stockings or tights can be used. On the plain side of the card draw a bold outline around the outside edge of the picture you have chosen. Mark dots all round the outline about $\frac{3}{8}''$ (1cm) apart. Pierce holes through the dots.

Using knitting wool or yarn, or thick embroidery cotton or silk, with a tapestry needle, a small child can sew in and out of the holes.

Transferring patterns

To use the card as a transfer, make the holes closer together. Place the card onto your material, hold it firmly and rub some powdered chalk through the holes. Lift the card carefully and you will find you have an outline of dots which you can draw in carefully with a chalk pencil and then embroider.